Marco,

May the angels lead you
always to your divine
destination.

Abide in Him always.

Much love,

Andrea B.

The

PAINTING ANGEL

Collection

The Ministry of Angels and

A Testament to the Greater Purpose of the Artist

Andrea Beloff

First Edition

ISBN: 978-1-937449-43-8 (hardcover, English)
ISBN: 978-1-937449-44-5 (e-book, English)
ISBN: 978-1-937449-45-2 (hardcover, Spanish)
ISBN: 978-1-937449-46-9 (e-book, Spanish)

Published by:

CELESTINE OPUS
ASHEVILLE, NORTH CAROLINA

(NKJV) Scripture quotations taken from The Holy Bible, New King James Version® NKJV®
Copyright © 1973, 1978, 1984, 2011 by Biblica, Inc.®
Used by permission. All rights reserved worldwide.

Celestine Opus books may be purchased in bulk for educational, fund-raising, business, or sales promotional use. For more information, please contact Books@CelestineOpus.com or toll-free 888-693-9365. Celestine Opus is an imprint of YAV Publications. Visit CelestineOpus.com

Author Contact information

Andrea Beloff Fine Art
PO Box 416398
Miami Beach, FL 33141
USA

www.PaintingAngels.live
www.AndreaBeloff.com
@andreabeloff
@andreabeloff_fineart

1 3 5 7 9 10 8 6 4 2

Published November 2019

Printed and Assembled in the United States of America

Reviews

"The Holy Spirit of God totally shows His children how much we are loved and protected through giving His Angels charge over us. Andrea Beloff's paintings and scriptures are such a gift to us. You can feel and see God's presence in her paintings and in her book. Thank you Andrea for allowing God to lead you and for blessing us through your work."

— Marlene Miller

"Your journey and transformation opened divine communication and revelation to your life purpose, through your work. In turn, reading your book awakened insight into my personal connection with the divine and revealed my own purpose."

— Brenda Marquez

Table of Contents

With deep gratitude and humility,

I honor our Heavenly Father, the Almighty God,

our Savior Jesus Christ,

and the anointing of the Holy Spirit.

They have blessed me indeed!.

THE PAINTING ANGEL
ART COLLECTION

I invite you to learn how I have come to paint the angels around me. These hosts of Heaven became an integral part of a new direction that my artistic career took starting in the Fall of 2014. My history includes 25 years in Santa Barbara, CA, as a dedicated paper-maker, using the traditional Japanese method in a highly detailed and textured tropical genre, that was particular to me.

Following this significantly successful phase, came a collapse and a long period of reflection through an eight-year life-induced sabbatical. During this time, I was broken, overwhelmed and confronted with true spiritual growth and emotional healing. I mixed mediums like never before and worked through many issues with my God given talent: art.

Once in Miami, I generated a very unique body of work titled, "The Love and Abundance Series." It was my testimony to the new Christian I had become and what that meant. The next step in my path shook me up the most: feeling lost in Miami and not experiencing meaningful positive results.

My tiny downtown studio was set up for oil painting, and I tackled my love for abstract art that had been a desire of mine since my studio days at the *Accademia di Belle Arti* in Venice, Italy. The rhythmic strokes took me into the most beautiful kaleidoscopic world of spiritual richness and renewal, filled with Biblical foundation. Immediately, I found heavenly bliss! Prayer guided me, and the palette knives interpreted my petitions.

The invisible realm of angels emerged almost immediately. I felt their "presence." This first body of work was so remarkable, it felt like an anointing of the Holy Spirit. The unworldliness of God was shaping me. This special time, returning to oil painting and sharing what transpired, was purposed for His glory, and to share about this unseen creation He uses.

I am forever grateful for this revelation of the Angels as a blessing, alongside my paintings. God is working through me. Until September 2019, the angels continued to pour out in a divine fashion. This spiritual gift came with tangible liveliness and with valuable information worth sharing. My life had new meaning.

The Presence of An Invisible World

The angels comforted me as they witnessed my lonely struggle and daily longing to examine the way Jesus' great salvation found expression in my life. In my tiny cubicle, on the 2nd floor of McCormick Place, an old eight-story building that housed artist studios, with a window overlooking a downtown Miami freeway, I would break down crying and plead that God would provide a new direction in my art and life.

I felt the presence of something I couldn't wrap my head around...like an invisible party. I wrestled with my pain, practiced the songs we would sing at Church on the worship team, (What an honor!) and painted away. There was relief in this daily practice. I cultivated spiritual dependence and an intimate relationship to my Creator, first and foremost. I would gradually soar to extreme heights of exhilaration. Second, it generated my breakthrough into contemporary art.

I explored the rich layered look of rhythmic palette knife painting techniques using oil paints on canvas as my medium. I played and played and played with this. I would place my paints from the tube onto acid free disposable palette sheets and mix the colors, lift the silky, luscious paints, and apply them to my canvas.

After a session, I couldn't figure out what excited me more...the painting or the mix of leftover paint on the palette! The palettes became studies, doodles, treasures filled with angelic imagery of the unseen world and revelations. One by one, an angel would emerge. They reflected the themes I painted on. Healing. Joy. Faith. Perseverance. Guidance. Hope. Prayer. Compassion. Guardianship. The spiritual battle between good and evil. Light and dark. Victory. Spiritual revival, and End Times...to name the greater part.

A completely new body of work emerged. Angel art was all over the studio. The painted angels as by-products of my paintings became proof of the interaction between the visible and the invisible realms. The artwork erupted with a passion and strength unparalleled to anything I had ever experienced. The revelation of these angels was indeed purposeful and instrumental in understanding how the Lord works omnisciently.

From this perspective, I share these visual declarations of this invisible world, bringing awareness of the existence and ministry of angels in the world today as stated in the Bible. God has a purpose, and He has a plan, and we are a part of it.

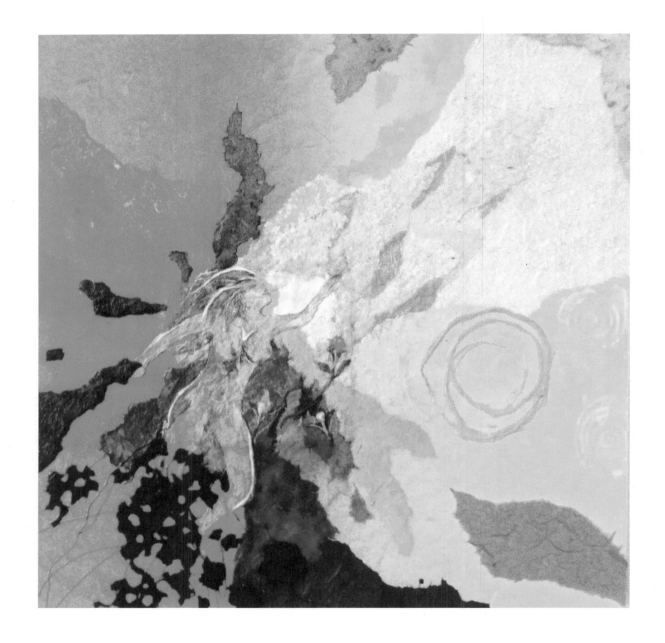

SURRENDER

The act of surrendering the navigation controls of one's life was one of the more complex experiences I had to undergo to realign my path according to God's will.

I was drowning in an ocean of ideas that impeded my creative release and that prompted me to stop trying to figure it out myself or through the ways of the world. To prepare myself for the rescue I so desperately sought, I asked that God's will be done in all areas of my life, including where my art would be headed.

I was ready to let go of my precious collaging technique of 25 years, and **SURRENDER**, the artwork, was among the last collages to be completed. I could sense this would be a letting go in so many ways. It was one of my life's hardest lessons but I wanted God to take control of the helm. I was submerged in a feeling of helplessness, unaware that God already had me on his life-line and was reeling me in close to Him. Clearly, I needed the Lord's intervention and He agreed: I was ready!

Romans 12:2

And be not conformed to this world: but be transformed by the renewing of your mind, that you may prove what is that good and acceptable, and perfect will of God.

Excited about the destination...   ETERNITY

One thing I could never give up is making art—it's my God-given gift, and through it, I address my reality. I have used my art for emotional and spiritual healing and confronted hard situations with it. I learned to love and sing praises to God through painting. For my needs and worries, I cry to him, and I paint to thank Him for always being there. The communication we share is often immediate, and together we play and laugh. This defines my relationship with God and my process of spiritual maturity, and when called upon to be renewed, resistance is useless. I embrace my every challenge with new perspective, and I am joyful and at peace when spiritually connected to Him.

Romans 8:28-29

And we know that all things work together for good to those who love God, to those who are called according to His purpose. For whom He foreknew, He also predestined to be conformed to the image of His Son, that He might be the firstborn among many brethren.

PAINTING ANGEL I

Luke 12:8-9

"Also I say to you, whoever confesses Me before men, him
the Son of Man also will confess before the angels of God.
But he who denies Me before men will be denied before
the angels of God."

Reading the history of our forefathers in the Bible reveals how God works. Seeing His hand woven into their lives gives us examples of His process, His right timing, and the victory that comes from being close to Him and His will. Theology classes helped deepen my understanding. I had developed a closeness to our creator and encouraged others to experience this relationship, and see how the stories repeat themselves. I was in awe of this awareness and wanted to talk about it with everyone, and I did, or I tried.

I had a dream that a friend of mine was gasping to be saved from the depths of the sea, and I interpreted it with the joy that comes from knowing that another of God's children would be renewed in the Lord. I shared it and went off to the studio and painted about the JOY of salvation described in the parable of the lost sheep. At that same time, the **PAINTING ANGEL I** would surface on the wax palette sheet upon which I mixed my paint. This Angel around me witnessed my joy and would make her joy visible to me as well. I was not rejoicing alone.

Luke 15:10

"In the same way, I tell you, there is rejoicing in the
presence of the angels of God over one sinner who repents."

THE WARRIOR ANGEL

THE WARRIOR ANGEL mimics the fervor of my desire to find my way through life and through painting. As I was working through issues and painting out my prayers, I was open to receive the inner strength and guidance to persevere without giving up what I knew was right in the eyes of the Jesus. Faith, strength, and self control were the operative words, and beyond that, the Lord knew I was ripe for the revelation of His angels, and they began to show up fast and furiously.

THE WARRIOR ANGEL shows up early in the revelation of angels. At first glance, he looked to me like an Apache Chief, and in time, I came to understand each element of the Armor of God that is required to have the readiness to stand against our adversary.

Matthew 26:53

"Or do you think that I cannot now pray to My Father, and He will provide Me with more than twelve legions of angels?"

Spiritual growth can be painful and living in this world with the evil forces of darkness even harder, but God reminds us that He goes before us and will fight for us. He tells us not to be anxious for anything and for everything to pray. Details on the Armor of God are revealed up ahead.

Philippians 4:6-7

Be anxious for nothing, but in everything by prayer and supplication, with thanksgiving, let your requests be made known to God; and the peace of God, which surpasses all understanding, will guard your hearts and minds through Christ Jesus.

ANGEL OF LOVE

In everything that applies to a Christlike behavior, *Love* is the most important.

ANGEL OF SONG

Psalm 13:5-6

But I have trusted in Your mercy;
My heart shall rejoice in Your salvation.
I will sing to the Lord,
Because He has dealt bountifully with me.

1 Corinthians 13:2

And though I have
the gift of prophecy, and
understand all mysteries and
all knowledge, and though I
have all faith,
so that I could
remove mountains,
but have not love,
I am nothing.

Colossians 3:16

Let the word of Christ dwell in you richly in all wisdom,
teaching and admonishing one another
in psalms and hymns and spiritual songs,
singing with grace in your hearts to the Lord.

THE GUIDING ANGEL

Rhythmic painting at its highest vibration emerges after praying for new direction in life and art.

Still, at the beginning stages of oil painting, I wondered what I was doing, where I was going; the internal struggle was real. I was too lost to steer my own ship. I wasn't even a ship.... I was so out of place, so alone, so uncertain of my future. What I did have was a strong relationship with God. I knew He was present but I didn't know the plan. I painted while asking for guidance, direction, a destination, a clear vision, and I received the oil painting that would show my purpose, appropriately titled INTO THE FUTURE...walking towards the light and inspiring people along the way, and on my painting palette, **THE GUIDING ANGEL** appeared.

To me, this interaction of question and response was simply amazing. I knew He had gone above and beyond any expectation I may have had. This was yet another time that God was there speaking to me so sincerely. I was beside myself in awe and in humility that He was so close and spoke so clearly, and that I understood. This was a supernatural exchange. There was nothing grounded or earthly about it. This was the kind of relationship and authority that I could trust and give my entire self to. Nothing in life gave me this much certainty, joy, meaning, love, wisdom, and protection. This is our God people! He is there for all of us, when we truly ask for Him.

2 Timothy 2:19

Nevertheless the solid foundation of God stands, having this seal: "The Lord knows those who are His," and, "Let everyone who names the name of Christ depart from iniquity."

Habakkuk 3:19

The Lord God is my strength; He will make my feet like deer's feet, And He will make me walk on my high hills.

ANGEL IN CLARITY

The year 2014 was coming to a close, and it became a routine to set an intention, through painting, for the New Year ahead.

This new direction in my life was wonderful but unfamiliar, nevertheless. My wish was that the path in front of me be as crystal clear as possible, so I could stay aligned in God's purpose. I sought clarity for each step.

It became imperative to stay sharp and aware, open and still. The interaction between my Father and I was developing, and I longed to hear Him and seek His will.

Numbers 24:4

The utterance of him who hears the words of God,
Who sees the vision of the Almighty,
Who falls down, with eyes wide open.

ANGEL and BARRIERS

Acts 7:53

ANGEL of UNION

Luke:20:34-36

ANGEL of COMPASSION

2 Chronicles 30:9

The next round of ANGELS continued to bring forth information through their behavior and assignments; they are God's humble servants and joyfully fulfill their tasks, whether great or small. Do we trust God, knowing that He will never take us where He won't be there with us? Our faith is continually tested and so it is with angels. *Angels must obey God.*

Psalm 103:20

Bless the Lord, you His angels,
who excel in strength,
who do his word,
heeding the voice His word.

1 Peter 5:6-7

Romans 1:20

1 Thessalonians 4:16

We learn from angels as they provide helpful examples for us to imitate, especially in how they worship God. The higher ranking angels, archangels, lead a great angelic army and wage war against demonic forces. They carry out some of God's judgments, bring plagues, and some angels even take on human form to undertake important visits. They are strong, powerful, and intelligent beings with moral judgment. Whenever we need them, God sends them, in all kinds of circumstances.

ANGEL in HUMILITY

ANGEL in NATURE

ANGEL of FORWARD MOVEMENT

THE ANGEL OF THE LORD

After the first dozen angels manifested, I was a little perplexed that I was now painting angels. Then, this one spoke differently to me. The title came to me right away, and seeing how it is used in Scripture, I came to know it was the Lord Himself.

The message was important too. Even though God was revealing angels to me, it never felt right praying to them. The angel speaking to John, in the Book of Revelations, warns him not to worship him. Worshiping angels would be a false doctrine.

We are to pray only to God, through Jesus, and to the Holy Spirit who alone are omniscient and can hear all His people's prayers at once.

Revelation 19:10

And I fell at his feet to worship him. But he said to me, "See that you do not do that! I am your fellow servant, and of your brethren who have the testimony of Jesus. Worship God! For the testimony of Jesus is the spirit of prophecy."

Matthew 11:29-30

"Take My yoke upon you and learn from Me, for I am gentle and lowly in heart, and you will find rest for your souls. for My yoke is easy and My burden is light."

1 Timothy 2:5

For there is one God and one Mediator between God and men, the Man Christ Jesus,

THE SECOND COMING

Long ago, we were warned about Jesus' second coming. It will be a time where believers will live with Jesus and God Himself in the New Jerusalem. The prophesies of the Bible are actually playing out ,and Satan's diabolical attempt at extortion of power is being revealed. Many people are awakening to hidden truths, and countries are revolting at such abuses. There is more emphasis being spoken of and written about Jesus's return, and the need for repentance for salvation. The time is short and we must share the Gospel. There is a great revival happening now.

In the Bible, we read that Daniel first interprets the dream that deeply disturbed King Nebuchadnezzar, the dream about what happens during these final days. Jesus shared about this with his disciples at the Last Supper and asked them to spread His teachings along with the crucial announcement about what will transpire in the End Times.

I can't help but feel the need to share about this too. It is important to see that our loved ones and others are saved. Many will be deceived unless they repent and take Jesus as their Lord and Savior. The alternative is horrendous—plagues will manifest, painful sores, terrible hail, the sun will scorch sinners with fire, and they will be left to die on the ground where birds will gorge on their flesh. These people will witness God's wrath and experience their first death. Then, they will be judged, and if their names do not appear in the Book of Life, they will be cast into the lake of fire, their second death.

Isaiah 13:9

Behold, the day of the Lord comes, cruel with both wrath and fierce anger, to lay the land desolate: and He will destroy its sinners thereof from it.

Isaiah 60:20

Your sun shall no longer go down, Nor shall your moon withdraw itself; For the Lord will be your everlasting light, And the days of your mourning shall be ended.

You should be praying that you be worthy of escaping before the tribulation times.

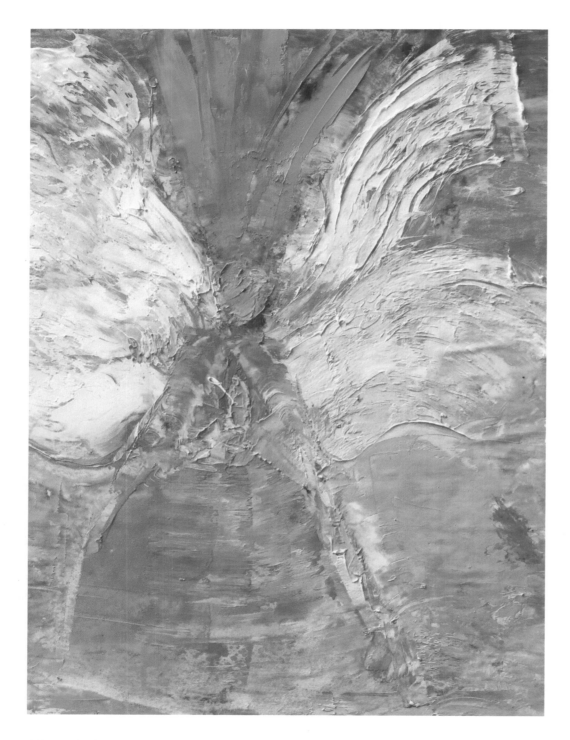

ANGEL IN PRAYER

Revelation 8:3-4

Then another angel, having a golden censer,
came and stood at the altar. He was given
much incense, that he should offer it with
the prayers of all the saints upon the
golden altar which was before the throne.
And the smoke of the incense,
with the prayers of the saints,
ascended before God
from the angel's hand.

Prayer is how we stay connected to the Lord, and angels also intercede bringing messages or delivering our prayers.

Matthew 18:19-20

"Again I say to you that if two of you agree on earth
concerning anything that they ask, it will be done for
them by My Father in heaven. For where two or three are
gathered together in My name, I am there
in the midst of them."

SPLENDOR OF AN ANGEL

David's Praise to God

1 Chronicles 29:10–13

Therefore David blessed the Lord before
all the assembly: and David said:

"Blessed are You, Lord God of Israel,
our Father, forever and ever.
Yours, O Lord, is the greatness,
The power and the glory,
The victory and the majesty;
For all that is in heaven
and in earth is Yours;
Yours is the kingdom, O Lord, And
You are exalted as head over all.
Both riches and honor come from You,
And You reign over all.
In Your hand is power and might;
In Your hand it is to make great
And to give strength to all.
Now therefore, our God,
We thank You
And praise Your glorious name."

Overjoyed and grateful for the renewed spiritual path I was now on, I wanted to paint about the grandeur of our God. He was full of grace at a time when I was giving up hope, and in His eyes, I was worthy. He made me more worthy than I could ever imagine. My joy spilled over to my art, and blessed are the days that I can paint and reflect about Him in my humble way.

The Angels around Him emanated beautiful light and sparkle, and many became visible at this time. I remember it well. I was still going through hard times, but I knew for a fact that my Almighty Father, Son Jesus, and the Holy Spirit were in my life forever.

I trusted Him because what He had already revealed was more than I had dared to imagine. To have this new direction meant everything to me. I was on a mission for Him and for those who may be touched by my work.

SPARKEY

SPARKEY is a superhero-like angel!

No one is really immune to the evil that lurks at every corner, and many of us are not taught about the spiritual realm. If our parents are unaware of this, we traverse our lives more vulnerable than necessary. Even many children who have grown up in Christ-led households, do not realize that the evil spirits are waiting to catch them off guard and lead them into temptation, rebellion, and away from God. As a parent, we must pray protection against these demons, over our children and loved ones, and we must educate ourselves in the authority given to us through Christ Jesus to rebuke Satan.

I have encountered many people who do not like to talk about the existence of the devil, and I find that to be a mistake. In the Bible, God asks us to know our enemy. As a child, I learned the Ten Commandments at a Catholic Chapel School in São Paulo, Brasil, and good and evil weren't so hard to tell apart. Certainly, I sinned many times as I grew, and looking back, I came to repent profusely and understand the need to stay close to God and His Word. Jesus will forgive us when we truly feel remorse in our hearts. However, it is important to be constantly fed from the well.

Family life also gave me a glimpse of our sinful nature. Some childhood teachers showed me that being in authority doesn't make you a good person or leader. College was for learning, and there I traveled a narrower path and was blessed early to find my God-given gift that stirs others. Divorce showed me a side of people that I never knew possible. It became increasingly harder along the way, until I came crashing down to my knees in supplication, and came to know Jesus' salvation. It still took years to learn to navigate through life with greater wisdom and understanding of God's provision. I finally understand that Satan never sleeps, but I can testify that spiritual maturity and walking with the Lord is where we truly find that peace.

Isaiah 66:16

For by fire and by His sword
The Lord will judge all flesh;
And the slain of the Lord shall be many.

2 Thessalonians 1:7-8

…and to give you who are troubled rest with us when the Lord Jesus is revealed from heaven with His mighty angels, in flaming fire taking vengeance on those who do not know God, and on those who do not obey the gospel of our Lord Jesus Christ.

ANGEL
in the
BATTLE ZONE

Matthew 13:41-42

"The Son of Man will send out His angels, and they will gather out of His kingdom all things that offend, and those who practice lawlessness, and will cast them into the furnace of fire. There will be wailing and gnashing of teeth."

PROTECTING ANGEL

Matthew 13:49

"So it will be at the end of the age. The angels will come forth, separate the wicked from among the just."

HEALING ANGEL

The Word of God is medicine to our flesh!

Proverbs 4:20-22

My son, give attention to my words; Incline your ear to my sayings. Do not let them depart from your eyes; Keep them in the midst of your heart; For they are life to those who find them, And health to all their flesh.

Revelation 22:1-2

And he showed me a pure river of water of life, clear as crystal, proceeding from the throne of God and of the Lamb. In the middle of its street, and on either side of the river, was the tree of life, which bore twelve fruits, each tree yielding its fruit every month. The leaves of the tree were for the healing of the nations.

Warfare Prayer

Ephesians 1:17-22, 2:4-6, 6:11-12, 14-17

…that the God of our Lord Jesus Christ, the Father of glory, may give to you the spirit of wisdom and revelation in the knowledge of Him, the eyes of your understanding being enlightened; that you may know what is the hope of His calling, what are the riches of the glory of His inheritance in the saints, and what is the exceeding greatness of His power toward us who believe, according to the working of His mighty power which He worked in Christ when He raised Him from the dead and seated Him at His right hand in the heavenly places, far above all principality and power and might and dominion, and every name that is named, not only in this age but also in that which is to come.

And He put all things under His feet, and gave Him to be head over all things to the church, which is His body, the fullness of Him who fills all in all. Thank you Lord for delivering me out of the darkness and into the light.

But God, who is rich in mercy, because of His great love with which He loved us, even when we were dead in trespasses, made us alive together with Christ (by grace you have been saved), and raised us up together, and made us sit together in the heavenly places in Christ Jesus,

Put on the whole armor of God, that you may be able to stand against the wiles of the devil. For we do not wrestle against flesh and blood, but against principalities, against powers, against the rulers of the darkness of this age, against spiritual hosts of wickedness in the heavenly places. I will put on the whole armor of God so I can withstand the evil day, having done all, to stand.

Stand therefore, having girded your waist with truth, having put on the breastplate of righteousness, and having shod your feet with the preparation of the gospel of peace; above all, taking the shield of faith with which you will be able to quench all the fiery darts of the wicked one. And take the helmet of salvation, and the sword of the Spirit, which is the word of God; praying always with all prayer and supplication in the Spirit, being watchful to this end with all perseverance and supplication for all the saints—

Our prayer life with the Lord is our greatest strength, as spelled out in Verse 18. Our prayer must be as intense as our fighting because prayer is fighting. Keep in mind, too, the wellbeing of the army as it includes your own wellbeing. In addition, cover everyone with the blood of Jesus. Since Jesus died for our sins, we now have access to enter the Holiest of Holies by way of His great sacrifice. Surrender yourself to Him. Refuse to be discouraged.

Honor Him that He is the God of all hope. Claim the victory of the resurrected Jesus and over the satanic forces in your life. Know that you have been given authority over Satan. Pray this in the Name of the Lord Jesus Christ with thanksgiving. Thanksgiving is important because your names have been written in the Book of Life! A reason to rejoice and seal it with an Amen.

ANGEL OF LIGHT I

ANGEL of PEACE, LOVE, and LIGHT

Revelation 10:1

I saw still another mighty angel coming down from heaven, clothed with a cloud. And a rainbow was on his head, his face was like the sun, and his feet like pillars of fire.

Matthew 5:9

"Blessed are the peacemakers, for they shall be called sons of God."

ANGEL ON HIGH

Zechariah 3:7

"Thus says the Lord of hosts: 'If you will walk in My ways, and if you will keep my command, then you shall also judge My house, and likewise have charge of My courts; and I will give you places to walk among these who stand here.

THE COURTS OF HEAVEN

The spiritual journey I walk has been master-crafted by the Lord Jesus Christ, Himself. He has led me through hard trials but also brought me to amazing people, with rich knowledge, with abounding experience, willing to share, when the time was right. Among these was my hairdresser, Gail, who introduced me to Robert Henderson's teachings on The Courts of Heaven. I have been to earthly courts during multiple custody battles over my children. These were led by absurdities; some won, some lost, and most were unfair. I wish I knew then that the devil has legal rights in the Courts and how he uses our sins and those of our ancestors to curse our lives without respite. In the eyes of the Lord, the timing must have been right. I was getting discouraged with so much adversity.

To enter the Courts of Heaven, you must ask to be put in remembrance. You must know what your prophetic destiny is as the Lord gave us grace and purpose before the beginning of time. Your prophetic destiny is something you enjoy, and it stirs you. You were created with gifts to accomplish it, are successful at it, and are also remunerated. You will have the people you need to accelerate your process. Then, you enter the Courts of Heaven and present your case. You remind the Lord what's in the Book and of the Covenant we have with Him through the blood of Jesus. Remind Him what you did for Him and the afflictions you went through because you belonged to Him. Repent of any and all sins when you don't know what the case is against you, only that something is resisting or impeding you. Mention that when you came to know Jesus and repented of your sins, the debts and hostile cases against you were canceled. Jesus took these out of the way and nailed them to the cross. Clear anything in your bloodline that may be brought against you. Ask that such legal rights be revoked. If there is something specific, bring it into awareness. Finally, ask to be acquitted.

I did this three times and had a breakthrough. I believe faith plays a huge part in receiving breakthroughs, as well. Your result will match your faith. It is written in Romans 10:17 "so then faith comes by hearing, and hearing by the Word of God." Enter to the Courts of Heaven as often as needed.

ANGEL IN FAITH

In heaven, as on earth, the Lord's will is done by angels, on command, with joy, and without question. They delight in being God's humble servants. They also find the greatest of joy to worship God continuously, particularly the seraphim, who are around His throne. They are examples for us to imitate. The difference, however, of who we are to the Lord, our God, is very important. To us He says, we are His friends and that He would lay His life down for us, if we follow His righteous commands.

Jesus says to us in Mark 11:22, "Have faith in God." When we pray, our faith must coincide with the desires of our heart. In Mark 11:24, He says "Therefore I say to you, whatever things you ask when you pray, believe that you receive them, and you will have them."

When the magnitude of Jesus' words reach your spirit, a light will go off, and you will be as if in another dimension. Your heart will resonate and sing in awe. God's angels are there delivering our prayers according to our faith and at the right time. Have more faith. Declare that you trust God and thank Him, for that relationship is the one he craves the most with us, and we should too. He is truly a most wondrous Living God. He makes us alive!

Isaiah 6:3

And they were calling to one another: "Holy, holy, holy is the Lord of hosts; the whole earth is full of His glory."

John 15:13-14

"Greater love has no one than this: then to lay down one's life for his friends. You are My friends if you do what I command you."

Mark 9:23

Jesus said to him,
"If you can believe, all things are possible to him who believes."

Psalm 91

He who dwells in the secret place of the Most High
Shall abide under the shadow of the Almighty.
I will say of the Lord, "He is my refuge and my fortress;
My God, in Him I will trust."
Surely He shall deliver you from the snare of the fowler
And from the perilous pestilence.
He shall cover you with His feathers, And under His wings you shall
take refuge; His truth shall be your shield and buckler.
You shall not be afraid of the terror by night,
Nor of the arrow that flies by day,
Nor of the pestilence that walks in darkness,
Nor of the destruction that lays waste at noonday.
A thousand may fall at your side, And ten thousand at your right
hand; But it shall not come near you.
Only with your eyes shall you look,
And see the reward of the wicked.
Because you have made the Lord, who is my refuge,
Even the Most High, your dwelling place,
No evil shall befall you,
Nor shall any plague come near your dwelling;
For He shall give His angels charge over you,
To keep you in all your ways.
In their hands they shall bear you up,
Lest you dash your foot against a stone.
You shall tread upon the lion and the cobra, The young lion and the
serpent you shall trample underfoot.
"Because he has set his love upon Me,
therefore I will deliver him;
I will set him on high,
because he has known My name.
He shall call upon Me, and I will answer him;
I will be with him in trouble; I will deliver him and honor him.
With long life I will satisfy him, And show him My salvation."

ANGEL IN FLORIDA

I moved to Florida in 2012, and it did feel more like home, as I am multicultural. I don't miss the California earthquakes and fires, their current policies, and gas prices! However, the hurricanes are still very unsettling for me! Looking forward to what's next as God assured me, "your home would be yours forever."

HERE

The Lord reveals Himself powerfully during the painting of **HERE**. It was the final painting from the *Journey Home Series* that evolved in the last month that my dad was terminal. When the Lord is looking to rekindle with His people, the miracles are continuous. So it was during that time, and my dad would come to know there was a great Presence in my life and in my home, and that God was greatly there for him as well. Ever more, during the final month, the Lord held me ever so close and comforted me during what I always anticipated would be the most difficult experience of my life—letting go of my dad. God's plan, however, was perfect. When I wasn't in the hospital or nursing facility, He would hold my attention in my painting process. I would feel no pain, and I would not go dark. He would not let me fall apart. The linear lined artwork was a physical expression of His pouring love, and it would continue to be a major element in much of my paintings. The revelation seemed even greater though, and Luke 9:27 brought it home:

But I tell you truly, there are some standing here who shall not taste death till they see the kingdom of God.

Philippians 1:4-6

always in every prayer of mine making request for you all with joy, for your fellowship in the gospel from the first day until now, being confident of this very thing, that He who has begun a good work in you will complete it until the day of Jesus Christ;

VICTORY ANGEL I

VICTORY ANGEL II

The **VICTORY ANGELS I** and **II** were a sweet surprise. They were like a gift from above. Something about them brought me hope and comfort that the road ahead of me wouldn't be as bleak as I had anticipated after my dad died. I still mourn his departure and weep like a baby, but once I settle down, a deep love comes as a result. If you have ever loved and cared for a very demanding and stubborn parent on your own, you know what a big responsibility it is. *I had taught my dad to pray to God. I showed him what repentance looked like.* I practiced Biblical laws with him, and I think he saw a new person that secretly made an impression on him. Victory had many facets.

Psalm 129:2

"Many a time they have afflicted me from my youth;
Yet they have not prevailed against me.

1 John 5

1 Corinthians 15:54

So when this corruptible has put on incorruption, and this
mortal has put on immortality, then shall be brought to
pass the saying that is written:
"Death is swallowed up in victory."

The Greatest Revelation in my Art: During the year I took care of my dad, the revelations given me in painting were magnificent. I titled them *The Journey Home Series,* and it concluded with the painting, HERE, at a time the Lord knew I needed Him more than ever and **HERE** He was. The series can be seen on my website at www.AndreaBeloff.com. The **VICTORY ANGELS I** and **II** emerged from this experience.

Consolation from God: My father and I were very close. With all its flaws, this relationship was the closest I would know from a person hitherto. My love and admiration for him was great. This particular presence was revealed in this sketch occurred just a few weeks before the date of his passing: July 28, 2018. My last immediate relative was rapidly reaching the end of his life while in my care. The guilt inside me was a result of trying so hard to cure my father from cancer's silent crawl. The enemy took a turn and showed frightening and ravaging signs that terrified both of us. All I could do was endure and accept what was happening. The only place I could stand finding any consolation was in front of the large canvas upon which to reproduce this sketch into a large painting that was begging for me to start. I'm not one to start a project in the middle of emotional turmoil. In this case I was being led. I have learned to trust these signs when I feel paralyzed from outer situations.

How I felt His presence: I started by identifying the bright white matte space and knowing it was good. It quickly became a force that held me. This is when the Lord would reveal Himself and true consolation would take place. The art held my attention; it embraced my spirit and my heart, and it directed my mind. It did everything so that I would not collapse. A true example of God: His mysterious ways of making Himself known in a language only I would understand. The Lord often comes through when I am painting, but on this account, He held me HERE. HERE, HERE, HERE, and no where else. It was a large canvas and the amount of lines were endless like a long shower of love and comfort.

The painting takes people aback and with great reason. It was HERE where God revealed Himself to me in a way that is hard to describe. His presence was so strong, His grip was so tight, and the comfort was so real. The decline of dad's health was so painful to observe. My inability to part from my dad was crippling. The fight to keep him alive, to keep his spirits up and build his body back after he had let it decline so much, was so tough. He was stubborn and the disease consumed his energy. It took him to places that were dark, and often it dragged me there too.

The Greatest Gift and Lesson: Thank you God for the opportunity to love and care for my father during his last year of life and for being there (HERE) for me at the capacity that You were. Nothing and no one compares to the love You show me. Only You can heal. You are in command and that was most evident. My love and faith in You has grown stronger and stronger, deeper and deeper.

The Victory Angels I and II: The experiences with my earthly and Heavenly Fathers are priceless. The time to share and reflect on past occurrences was so valuable. Consolation, support, and guidance from God was a gift. Understanding that my responsibility as caregiver was complete and that my bigger assignments were yet to come was the VICTORY experienced through the message of the Angels. I feel privileged to share this part of my testimony.

IN COMMAND

For the record, it is not always an angel that comes as a revelation on my palettes. There is one message that surfaced at prominent times during this five-year period of painting the mystery of God's angels, and it was this: above anything that may be happening, Our Father God, is always in control, and He has a most distinct, timely, and supernatural way of making this known. The proofs of Him, through spirit operating in my life, were enough to bind my heart and my soul to Him above all things. I have lived a life where I could be alone with Him often, and I promise you, those have been my most meaningful moments ever. This Mystery of infinite capacity dwells in me, and the fact that He shows me this with unexpected imagery is beyond cool!

The sound of HERE was so loud and clear, and so comforting. **He Truly Was In Control**. All I could say at that moment of extreme overwhelming circumstances was, "I hear You. I hear You. Thank You for the reassurance at a time of much need."

Psalm 119:46-47

I will speak of Your testimonies also before kings,
And will not be ashamed.
And I will delight myself in Your commandments,
Which I love.

THE SOARING ANGELS I AND II

These Angels surfaced in December 2018, a trying time for Holidays after the last member of my family passes, and other difficulties arise. The Lord, however, persisted in encouraging me through revelation that His love was unfailing.

The **SOARING ANGELS** vibrate to the tunes of King David in Psalm 18, in which the Lord delivers him from the hand of all his enemies and from the hand of Saul. As the Lord worked in my life, through faith and supplication, I felt the similitude of also being delivered from some of my enemies. The victories of staying close to the Lord and trusting in Him at all times are displayed in the boldness and courage of the energy of these angels resulting in greater spiritual heights. All the glory be to God. He is worthy of so much praise. I felt great strength during this time. I embarked on a project that resulted in a very supernatural experience. Sometimes, the first step is the hardest, but I took that step, and God met me one-hundredfold. My faith was rewarded.

FIREWORKS of 2019

This artwork painted on January 1st, 2019, forecasted that it would be a year full of sparks. Our Father God asks us to walk in the spirit of His light, so we can receive the anointing of the Holy Spirit and do all things through Christ who strengthens us. This year, if we could do this, God will use us to do His will. Our God is in control, and His hand will be revealed in ways that cannot be denied by those with eyes that see.

Matthew 5:14

You are the light of the world. A city that is set on a hill cannot be hidden.

This year, I have walked a more spirit-filled life than I ever have with the Lord Our God. It was a priority. I feel that I may look back on it and call it my best year ever. My prophetic artwork is going into the world, and all these angels that took five years to emerge in the form of art, has been essential for the completion of this book. I trust and pray it will be well received and far reaching. My faith has grown so much.

THE GUARDIANS

Luke 4:10-11

For it is written: 'He shall give His angels charge over you, to keep you,' and, in their hands they shall bear you up, lest you dash your foot against a stone.'

Psalm 3:8

Salvation belongs to the LORD
Your blessing is upon
Your people. Selah

There have been times throughout my walk in this life during which I have seen miraculous occurrences. I never saw an angel, as they are invisible, but I know they are obedient to God. I have been delivered by angels and by the Holy Spirit. Not too long ago, and in two flashes, my whole car and body were restored when we should have perished horribly. It was the most unbelievable experience that conforms only to the likes of a miracle. It is wise to reflect on such events and connect to this God force and remember not to be anxious for anything, for His will rules.

THE BREAKTHROUGH ANGELS I and II

Acts 12:8-11

Then the angel said to him, "Gird yourself and tie on your sandals"; and so he did. And he said to him, "Put on your garment and follow me." So he went out and followed him, and did not know that what was done by the angel was real, but thought he was seeing a vision. When they were past the first and the second guard posts, they came to the iron gate that leads to the city, which opened to them of its own accord; and they went out and went down one street, and immediately the angel departed from him.

And when Peter had come to himself, he said, "Now I know for certain that the Lord has sent His angel, and has delivered me from the hand of Herod and from all the expectation of the Jewish people."

ANGEL in a DREAM

Genesis 28:12-15

Then he dreamed, and behold, a ladder was set up on the earth, and its top reached to heaven; and there the angels of God were ascending and descending on it. And behold, the Lord stood above it and said: "I am the Lord God of Abraham your father and the God of Isaac; the land on which you lie I will give to you and your descendants. Also your descendants shall be as the dust of the earth; you shall spread abroad to the west and the east, to the north and the south; and in you and in your seed all the families of the earth shall be blessed. Behold, I am with you and will keep you wherever you go, and will bring you back to this land; for I will not leave you until I have done what I have spoken to you."

For all of you who know that I dream a lot: I'm not the only one who dreams, for this is another way God speaks to us. I get messages in dreams, when I paint, and when I pray. Here in this painting called **_KEEP WALKING_**, the message is about being steadfast, holding on to our faith, and knowing God's promises. His love is unfailing and His presence is constant. His plan was such that whoever believes in him shall not perish but have eternal life. We have so much to look forward to.

1 John 2:28

And now, little children, abide in Him, that when He appears, we may have confidence and not be ashamed before Him at His coming.

ANGEL OF THE REVIVAL

A sign of the End of Ages. A time of intense change and awakening in the world. Truths uncovered. Mysteries revealed. More significantly, an opportunity for spiritual revival in the hearts of those who hear His call. The Lord is pouring out His grace. The Holy Spirit is intensely at work, and upon receiving Jesus as our Lord and Savior, our eyes are unveiled, our sincere repentance clears our sins, and undeserving and not through works, we are renewed and given eternal life.

Psalm 80:18

Then we will not turn away from You;
revive us, and we will call upon Your Name.

Acts 4:12

Nor is there salvation in any other, for there is no
other name under heaven given among men by
which we must be saved."

ANGEL ON FIRE for the USA

Genesis 12:1-3

Promises to Abram
Now the Lord had said to Abram:
"Get out of your country, from your family
And from your father's house,
To a land that I will show you.
I will make you a great nation; I will bless you
And make your name great;
And you shall be a blessing.
I will bless those who bless you,
And I will curse him who curses you;
And in you all the families of the earth shall be blessed."

God's Judgment is handed out exactly by how we treat the Nation of God—Israel. History has proven this time and time again. In the Presidential Election of 2016, the raising up of leadership in the USA was achieved by God Himself; Mr. Donald J. Trump became President of the United States, creating a mindset of unbelief within the opposition. The judgment reflects exactly how our prior President, Obama, intervened in the election of Netanyahu. Our Living God is a just God.

On December 6, 2017, President Trump proclaimed Jerusalem to be the Capital of Israel, 70 years after President Truman recognized Israel as the Nation State of the Jewish people. This also marks the year of Jubilee, and ,every 50 years, the law of jubilees commands that the trumpet "shall sound throughout all your land." Ah ha! The US Senate acknowledged the 50th year and called for President Trump to recognize the right of the Jewish people to their ancestral possession, Jerusalem. This could only have been orchestrated by God for His purposes, and it blesses the US with precious time for spiritual revival and to boldly continue to share the Gospel as the End Times approach.

Micah 4:5

For all people walk each in the name of his god,
But we will walk in the name of the Lord our God
Forever and ever.

This powerful flame of fire,
ministering angel, brings forth God's Plan, a message of judgement, a legal way for His people to their Promised Land and additional time for spiritual revival.

ANGEL AWAITING JUDGMENT

It is written, we will judge the angels.

Angels have a place in God's purpose, and they needed to stay in obedience. Angels were never said to be made "in the image of God," as we humans are said to have been created, but they are equally moral and highly intelligent beings. It is written: "And the angels who did not keep their proper domain, but left their own abode, He has reserved in everlasting chains under darkness for the judgment of the great day"; (Jude 1:6). Nowhere does it say that Jesus died for the sins of angels. They are only temporarily above us in capacity.

2 Peter 2:4

For if God did not spare the angels who sinned, but cast them down to hell and delivered them into chains of darkness, to be reserved for judgment.

To better understand the difference between how God made humans, and how He made angels, it is written in Hebrews 2:7 that though "You have made him (mankind) a little lower than the angels, You have crowned him with glory and honor, and set him over the works of Your hands." When our salvation is complete we will be exalted above angels and rule over them.

1 Corinthians 6:3

Do you not know that we shall judge angels?

ANGEL OF THE RENAISSANCE

The Messiah spoke to the Apostles about the importance of spreading the Gospel to all nations as they would prepare the way for His Second Coming. The message of this angel is that Jesus is coming back for us, as He promised. During this Church Age, God leads us in spirit to salvation, as we **repent** and **believe with faith** that Jesus paid the price for our sins and canceled our debt at the Cross. We accept Jesus into our hearts, as Lord and Savior, and are reborn. This angel reminds us that God loves us so much, He is sending His Son back to get us. God is full of mercy, and He will pour His grace over His children who call upon the Name of the Lord. There will be a time that the Holy Spirit will no longer be present. We should encourage each other now about the peace that resides in those who believe. God longs for a relationship with each one of us, so that He can hear our petitions and answer our prayers. That time in spirit with Him will give us the joy and the peace our souls' crave. We call Him a Living God for this reason, because He makes known He is truly present, and His ways are supernatural. The words in the Bible are a great way to experience Jesus because the Father speaks through those words. The time to receive Jesus is now. This knowledge, understanding, and renewal of the spirit is what will make the difference in our lives and for all that is to come.

Matthew 11:28-30

"Come to Me, all you who labor and are heavy laden, and I will give you rest. Take My yoke upon you and learn from Me, for I am gentle and lowly in heart, and you will find rest for your souls. For My yoke is easy and My burden is light."

John 14:6

"Let not your heart be troubled; you believe in God, believe also in Me. In My Father's house are many mansions; if it were not so, I would have told you. I go to prepare a place for you. And if I go and prepare a place for you, I will come again and receive you to Myself; that where I am, there you may be also. And where I go you know, and the way you know. Thomas said to Him, "Lord, we do not know where You are going, and how can we know the way? "Jesus said to him, "I am the way, the truth, and the life. No one comes to the Father except through Me."

John 15:7

If you abide in Me, and my words abide in you, you shall ask what you will, and it shall be done unto you.

ANGEL of the REVIVAL For the NATIONS

The year 2019 turns out to be another year of great revelations about the purpose of angels through my art. Here is a glimpse of how they surface on my wax palette sheets. **ANGELS OF THE REVIVAL** proves to be the great theme of the moment as times become darker and the battle between good and evil is now ruthless and in plain sight. So many Painting Angels are pouring in on this inspiration as they fulfill God's purpose. Hallelujah! Divine help is at hand. Awakening is taking place all over the world. We must not take for granted or put aside for later, God's grace, as it is upon us now. People are rising in faith and committing their lives to Jesus and this assignment. Many are awakening to their divine destination and spreading the Gospel, into all nations, for all people. As many as are uncovering the lies and evil doings of major players, Our God keeps lifting His faithful ones to greater responsibilities and the uncovering of His Great Mysteries, and they are out of this world. Nothing is a coincidence, but the Bible also says that many will lose their faith. Guard your mind and remain in His Word so you may endure. You were created for such times as these. Stand strong.

Acts 11:16-18

Then I remembered the word of the Lord, how He said, 'John indeed baptized with water, but you shall be baptized with the Holy Spirit.' If therefore God gave them the same gift as He gave us when we believed on the Lord Jesus Christ, who was I that I could withstand God?" When they heard these things they became silent; and they glorified God, saying, "Then God has also granted to the Gentiles repentance to life."

Hebrews 11:6

But without faith it is impossible to please Him, for he who comes to God must believe that He is, and that He is a rewarder of those who diligently seek Him.

ANGELS of the REVIVAL
For the NATIONS

Abundance of rain is spiritual revival!

I have noticed, that sometimes, my palette knives just start to paint in a rhythmic fashion, like a pour, in synchronicity to a greater force. This happened vividly in various Revival themed works. It is amazing to see how God speaks His purpose, through the art; sometimes we are years away, at other times, it is exactly when He is at work worldwide. It is magical and an honor to be part of this experience. It makes me cry: *I Love you, Father Almighty. I'm here for you. Use me.*

1 Kings 18:41

There is a sound of abundance of rain.

It is so in the spiritual world. There are those who know of a coming Revival long before there is any sign. They have felt their prayers being answered, and have heard the cry of the penitent sinner, though, as yet, he seems to be as hard and careless as ever.

Joel 2:28

"And it shall come to pass afterward
That I will pour out My Spirit on all flesh;
Your sons and your daughters shall prophesy,
Your old men shall dream dreams,
Your young men shall see visions.

Isaiah 44:3

For I will pour water
on him that is thirsty,
and floods on the dry ground:
I will pour my spirit on your seed,
and my blessing on your offspring:

Let it pour in!

ANGEL IN AUTHORITY

It is at this time that
knowledge shall increase,
that we must stay
sober, strong, and faithful,
and share the Gospel,
and claim our victory
in Christ Jesus.

Luke 10:18-20,23

And He said to them,
"I saw Satan fall like lightning from heaven. Behold,
I give you the authority to trample on serpents and
scorpions, and over all the power of the enemy, and nothing
shall by any means hurt you. Nevertheless do not rejoice
in this, that the spirits are subject to you, but rather rejoice
because your names are written in heaven."

Then He turned to His disciples and said privately,
"Blessed are the eyes which see the things you see.

It is a time to repent and to walk deeply in spirit with the living God. It is good to adhere to the Sabbath as your day of resting in the Lord. He renews your mind and heart daily, if you let Him. Start your day praying for yourself, your children, and the army. Use the full armor of God, to stand in authority, against the enemy. Take opportunities to gather together, fast, pray, and use the full name of God, Lord Jesus Christ, during worship. Know that Scripture is your defense and take dominion over your mind as the enemy enters there only if you allow him. Remember that the struggle is not against flesh and blood but against rulers, powers of the dark world, and against spiritual forces of evil in the heavenly realms. And last but not least, be aware of your surroundings, be vigilant to occurrences happening in the world and especially how they relate to the Hebrew calendar. God's mysteries are being revealed.

THE DECEIVER

Satanic deception has been at work since the inception of man on earth. This rebellious being, who was cast out of Heaven, clearly tries to drift humanity away from God's commands and maneuver humanity away from knowing the Great Redeemer, Jesus Christ, who paid the price for their sins at the Cross where their own salvation lies. "Why?" You might ask. Because Satan wants to overrule God. He thinks that if all of God's people fail Him, Satan, himself, will have dominion over them.

Now that God has raised President Trump to lead the Nation and here we are fighting in God's battle, we also know that victory is ours in Christ Jesus. Hallelujah!

We must not be deceived. We must know our enemy, his evil ways, and be at peace that our great fight is won through the power and authority of Jesus Christ. We have been warned in the First and Great Commandment to love Our God above all else.

Mark 12: 29-31

Jesus answered him, "The first of all the commandments is: 'Hear, O Israel, the Lord our God, the Lord is one. And you shall love the Lord your God with all your heart, with all your soul, with all your mind, and with all your strength.' This is the first commandment. And the second, like it, is this: 'You shall love your neighbor as yourself.' There is no other commandment greater than these."

Luke 13:35

"See! Your house is left to you desolate; and assuredly, I say to you, you shall not see Me until the time comes when you say, 'Blessed is He who comes in the name of the LORD!'"

2 Corinthians 11:14

And no wonder! For Satan himself transforms himself into an angel of light.

Jesus in Hebrew is Yeshuah. I would love you to know Him.

Hebrews 1:14

Are they not all ministering spirits sent forth to minister for those who will inherit salvation?

John 1:17

For the law was given by Moses, but grace and truth came by Jesus Christ.

Jeremiah 30:3

For behold, the days are coming,' says the LORD, 'that I will bring back from captivity My people Israel and Judah,' says the LORD. 'And I will cause them to return to the land that I gave to their fathers, and they shall possess it.'

RAINING ANGELS

Let it rain spiritual revival over all nations...and receive Jesus.

As End Times draw near and the world turns upside down in front of our very eyes, I have come to understand that many people, and particularly many of the descendants of Israel, have not yet come to know and understand that Jesus Christ was the Son of God, and that God Himself laid His life down for them, and that He rose from the dead as proof that through Him, they shall inherit salvation and eternal life. Drawing near to God will be the end of Satan and the temptations that mislead so many to lose The Way. Oh God, I pray salvation for anyone who draws near You, as it is written that when they draw near, You will have great compassion. Gather your people from the ends of the earth to where they were scattered, and restore to them the land of their ancestors, prosper them, renew their hearts so they may love You deeply and have life everlasting. May You show Yourself greatly and help them to know your Son and the works of the Holy Spirit. May Your great mercy be theirs in the Name of Yeshuah, the Messiah.

God is Sovereign and does as He says throughout time.

Jerusalem is the Holy Land, the land of His people, the descendants of Abraham, Isaac and Jacob. This land includes the cities of Judah, and it was designated by God from the beginning, and He will restore it to His people as promised in the End Times.

Isaiah 1:24, 26

Therefore the Lord says,
The Lord of hosts,
the Mighty One of Israel,
"Ah, I will rid Myself
of My adversaries,
And take vengeance
on My enemies.

I will restore your judges as at
the first,
And your counselors
as at the beginning.
Afterward you shall
be called
the city of
righteousness,
the faithful city."

Jerusalem

Zechariah 2:8

For thus says the Lord of hosts: "He sent Me after glory, to the nations which plunder you; for he who touches you touches the apple of His eye.

1 Thessalonians 5:8-9

But let us who are of the day be sober, putting on the breastplate of faith and love, and as a helmet the hope of salvation. For God did not appoint us to wrath, but to obtain salvation through our Lord Jesus Christ.

ENTRANCE OF THE NEW JERUSALEM

God fulfills His promises. He keeps His Word and acts with Sovereignty where necessary. God has manifested in ways throughout time that there should be no doubt that He is the One and Only Mighty King of Kings, and we should fear Him. No one should fall away. For this reason, I urge you to be grafted onto the root, and receive the blessing promised to Abraham and his children. God's people will come together in Jerusalem from the ends of the world and He will bless those who come in the Name of the Lord. The entire world will be focused on Jerusalem, and Jesus will come back to the Mount of Olives in Jerusalem and restore them to Himself.

Romans 11:17

And if some of the branches were broken off, and you, being a wild olive tree, were grafted in among them, and with them became a partaker of the root and fatness of the olive tree.

Revelation 11:15

Then the seventh angel sounded: And there were loud voices in heaven, saying, "The kingdoms of this world have become the kingdoms of our Lord and of His Christ, and He shall reign forever and ever!"

Ezekiel 28:25-26

"Thus says the Lord God: 'When I have gathered the house of Israel from the peoples among whom they are scattered, and am hallowed in them in the sight of the Gentiles, then they will dwell in their own land which I gave to My servant Jacob. And they will dwell safely there, build houses, and plant vineyards; yes, they will dwell securely, when I execute judgments on all those around them who despise them. Then they shall know that I am the Lord their God.'"

ANGEL IN ACTION

This one, I believe to be my beautiful and mighty personal Angel, always acting along-side me, leading a pack and furthering my divine assignments. It is my desire to help awaken you to the spiritual realm through the Holy Word of God, magical palette knife paintings, and written revelations that mimicked my experiences. I didn't come up with of this all on my own. I have been guided. I am part of the plan. I am so grateful for the Angels and this journey.

"We have so much work to do," declares Andrea, the artist. "Our country needs us to be strong and united and so does the world. Already we are having to defend our faith and our right to express it. Our faith in Jesus and our knowledge that He is the only way to the Father must be sealed in our minds and bonded in our hearts."

Psalm 89:15

Blessed are the people who know the joyful sound!
They walk, O Lord, in the light of Your countenance.

DESCENDING ANGEL

Angel sculptures are starting to grace my art as well, and I long to write on other artistic revelations I have painted. For now, it is an honor to bring forth this information to you, and give you a glimpse of the invisible world of God's angels. I ask that His angels be with you for these unsettling but amazing times we live in, as we prayerfully await the return of our Lord Jesus Christ. May peace be in your heart.

If this book has salted your walk with the Lord and stirred in you a spirit into revival, I ask that you please share it with your family and friends. It is my desire to plant seeds of hope and salvation to anyone who has not yet received Jesus. End Times are here and we are in this together. I urge you to spend more time in your Bibles in which God has breathed His Word in order to move you in His direction. We are going home.

Revelation 22:20-21

He who testifies to these things says,
"Surely I am coming quickly."
Amen. Even so, come, Lord Jesus!
The grace of our Lord Jesus Christ
be with you all. Amen.

Oh, that You would bless me indeed, and enlarge my territory, that Your hand would be with me, and that You would keep me from evil.

CONCLUSION

I Praise You, God!
My heart sings praises to You Almighty One!
God is Our Father, Our Friend, and Our Judge.
He made us from dust and His Holy Breath.
He sent his Son to lay His life for us.
He left The Holy Spirit to be in us
and guide us.
God's Angels are everywhere!
They have been very busy playing an ongoing
part in God's plan of salvation for His people,
and I am so endeared to them
as they have filled my life,
the art scene, and been a blessing to others.
This brings me to the end of this book
where it must be said
that God did not create the angels to go
against Him and be forgiven.
Because we have endured
in His battle with the fallen angels,
His salvation plan is all for us.
But we will judge the angels, that we know.

Hebrews 2:16
For indeed He does not give aid to angels, but
He does give aid to the seed of Abraham.

He lives in me
and He will live in you,
through Jesus.
He has given me many more of these revelations
through art
as another means to tell His Story
and what is to come.
It has been a blessing and a joy
to live with this Art
reminding me of our journey together,
and it is available to you too.
I truly hope to show you more of the art
as I have painted about all of this.
It has been the richest, most fulfilling partnership,
one that moves me and hopefully stirs you too.
Thank you for your attention
And your support.

Andrea Beloff

Unraveling the Mysteries
of the Most High

This next compilation of artworks can be seen now on the website:

www.AndreaBeloff.com

INDEX

ABOUT THE AUTHOR

Andrea Beloff is a full time dedicated Painter and now also doing Angel Sculptures.
She lives in Miami and exhibits at Major Art Fairs in New York, Miami, and Internationally.

Andrea's work can be seen on her website, where she also maintains a Blog.
AndreaBeloff.com

The Angels have an exclusive section:
PaintingAngels.com
They are also available as Metallic Photo Reproductions behind acrylic and lovely Greeting Cards.

You are also welcome to sign up for her Newsletter through the website with your email.
Here, Andrea likes to share new art, tell stories about them and make little special offers.

Instagram is a great way to interact with Andrea:
@andreabeloff
@andreabeloff_fineart
Through Instagram she started a GLOBAL PRAYER Time at 9 a.m. and 9 p.m. EST where she posts about Global issues that warrant prayer.
Please join her in her effort to make a difference as a Prophetic Artist.

Andrea Beloff
P.O. Box 416398
Miami Beach, FL 33141
USA

AndreaBeloff4@gmail.com

CPSIA information can be obtained
at www.ICGtesting.com
Printed in the USA
BVHW091020171119
563918BV00002B/2/P